The Jataka Tales

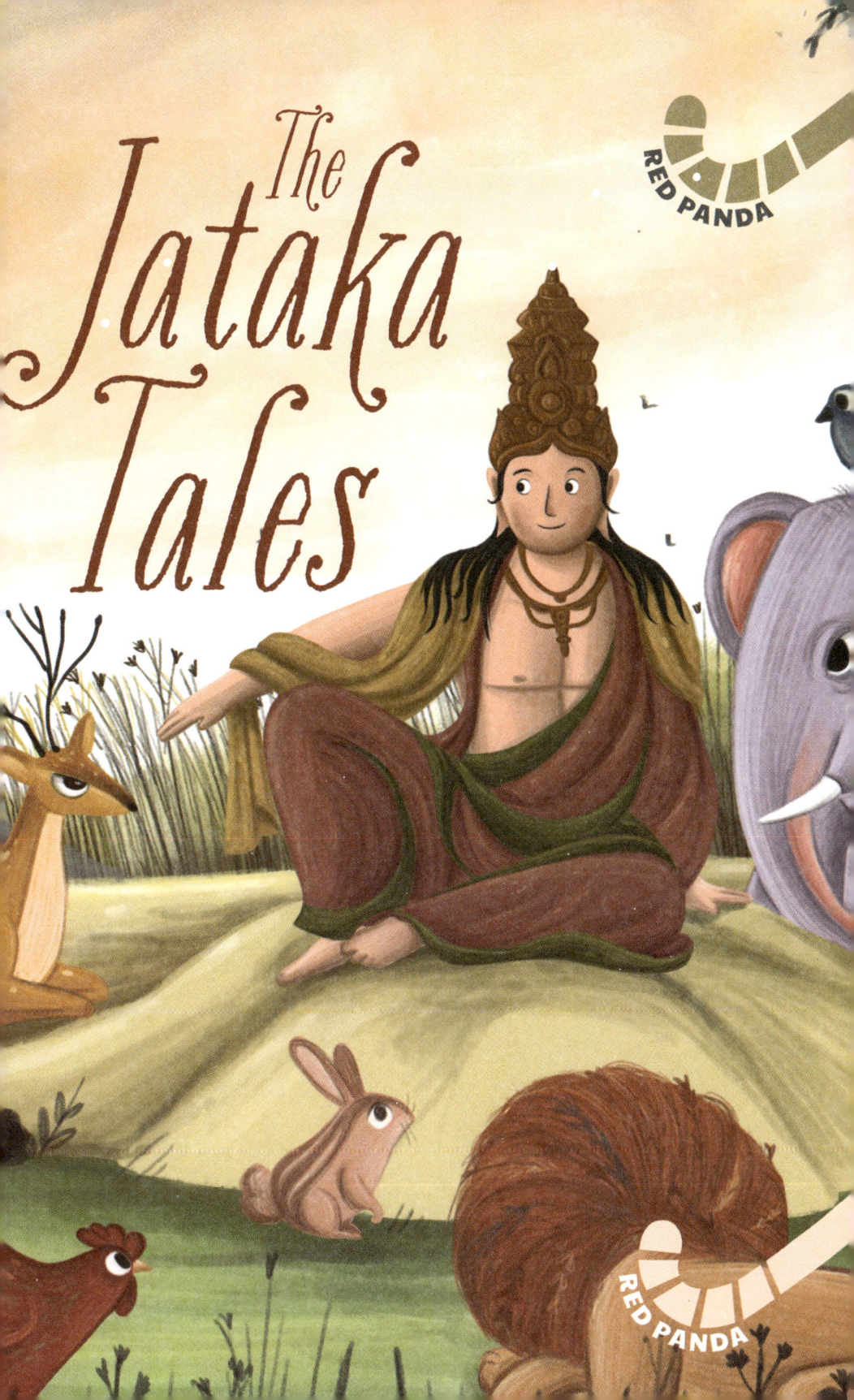

Published by Red Panda, an imprint of Westland Books, a division of Nasadiya Technologies Private Limited, in 2025

No. 269/2B, First Floor, 'Irai Arul', Vimalraj Street, Nethaji Nagar, Alapakkam Main Road, Maduravoyal, Chennai 600095

Westland, the Westland logo, Red Panda and the Red Panda logo are the trademarks of Nasadiya Technologies Private Limited, or its affiliates.

Text and illustrations © Nasadiya Technologies Private Limited, 2025

ISBN: 9789371979795

10 9 8 7 6 5 4 3 2 1

This is a work of fiction. Names, characters, organisations, places, events and incidents are either products of the author's imagination or used fictitiously.

All rights reserved

Book design by Pratik M. Kalekar

Printed at Parksons Graphics Pvt. Ltd

No part of this book may be reproduced, or stored in a retrieval system, or transmitted in any form or by any means, electronic, mechanical, photocopying, recording, or otherwise, without express written permission of the publisher.

WHAT ARE THE JATAKA TALES?

A long time ago in India, people loved telling stories about talking animals, wise kings, and regular folks making tough choices. These stories were fun to hear, but they also taught us to be kind, brave, honest and clever.

Among the most treasured of these are the Jataka Tales—stories from the many lives of Buddha. The Buddha was a great teacher who helped people live with peace and kindness. Before he became the Buddha, he lived many other lives.

In each of these lives, he was called the Bodhisatta (say: *bo-dhi-sat-ta*), which means someone who is on a journey to become a Buddha. Sometimes the Bodhisatta was a kind deer, a clever monkey or a brave bird. Other times, he was a prince, a merchant or a simple villager. No matter who he was, the Bodhisatta always tried to do what was right, even when it was very hard.

Time and again, his kindness was noticed by Indra, the king of the gods. He often watched from the heavens and sometimes tested the Bodhisatta to see how kind and wise he truly was.

People shared these stories to remind one another that being good, even in small ways, can change the world. Now, we begin our journey through the many lives of the Bodhisatta.

CONTENTS

1. THE MONKEYS AND THE WATERING CANS — 1

2. THE LITTLE QUAIL AND THE BIG NET — 7

3. THE RAIN OF RICHES — 12

4. THE TREE THAT WAS NOT A MANGO — 17

5. THE BRAVE PRINCE AND THE FOREST OGRE — 22

6. THE FOOLISH PRICE MAKER — 27

7. THE TALE OF AVISHYA THE UNSHAKEN — 32

8. THE CLEVER CROW — 37

9. THE DEER WHO PLAYED DEAD — 42

10. THE LOTUS ROOTS — 47

11. THE BRAVE LITTLE PARROT — 52

12. THE PARTRIDGE WHO PLANTED A TREE — 57

13. THE JACKAL AND THE RAT KING

62

14. THE JACKAL WHO TRIED TO ROAR

67

15. THE BOY WHO BROUGHT BACK A TIGER

72

16. THE PET ELEPHANT

77

17. THE OWL AS KING

82

18. THE FLIGHT OF THE BEASTS

87

19. THE CAT AND THE CLEVER COCK

92

20. THE BRAVE WHITE HORSE AND THE GOBLIN CITY

97

21. THE CHAMELEON'S BETRAYAL

102

22. THE TREE THAT TOLD A LIE

107

23. THE CARPENTER, THE SON, AND THE BODHISATTA
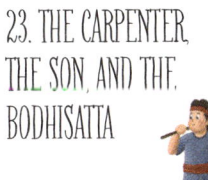
112

24. COURAGE AND KINDNESS

117

25. THE CLEVER CRAB AND THE CRANE

122

1. THE MONKEYS AND THE WATERING CANS

Once the Bodhisatta was born as a gentle man who wandered from town to town, teaching kindness and wisdom. One summer, he went strolling through city of Benares. It was festival time, and the city shone like a jewel on the riverbank.

Lanterns dangled from every rooftop, swaying in the warm breeze. Musicians played flutes and drums at every corner. The smell of mouth-watering sweets filled the air.

Even the king's gardener, who normally preferred the quiet of the royal garden, could not resist the cheer. He packed a small basket with mangoes and sweet rice cakes, and went off to join the festivities. Before leaving, he took one last look at the garden.

Rows of young saplings stood straight, planted in neat lines, their leaves trembling in the sunlight. The gardener frowned. 'I can't leave them like this,' he thought. 'They'll dry out in the heat. They're too young to be left alone.'

Just then he heard a rustling from the mango tree overhead. It was the monkey king, full of pride, chewing on a jackfruit pod.

He and his troop lived in the royal park, swinging from branch to branch, causing mischief now and then.

The gardener called up to him. 'Monkey king! Would you and your troop keep watch over the garden today? These young trees need watering while I'm away.'

The monkey king sat up tall. 'Of course we will,' he said, puffing out his chest. 'Leave it to us.'

The gardener smiled and handed him the watering cans. 'Not too much and not too little. Just enough to keep them growing well.'

With that, he strolled off to the city, humming a happy tune.

The monkey king clapped his hands. 'Gather round, everyone! We have been given an important duty. We must water the trees. But wisely!'

'What does wisely mean?' asked a young monkey, scratching his head.

'It means,' said the monkey king, 'we don't give all trees the same amount. Big roots need more water. Small roots need less.'

'But how do we know how big their roots are?' asked another.

The monkey king grinned. 'We'll pull up each tree and have a look!'

The troop cheered. They went around the garden and grabbed the saplings by their slim trunks, tugging them out of the ground one by one.

'Aha! This one has long roots—give it two cans!'

'Short roots here—just a sprinkle!'

THE MONKEYS AND THE WATERING CANS

Water splashed, mud flew and little trees lay scattered around.

Once the roots were watered, they pushed the trees back into the ground. But the trees wobbled. Some tilted sadly. Others couldn't stand at all. Their roots lay exposed, and their leaves began to curl.

By midday, the garden was in ruins. Muddy puddles and fallen petals filled the paths. Many of the young trees were broken or about to wither.

And that was when a calm voice came from the gate. 'What has happened here?'

It was the Bodhisatta, who had come walking through the garden on his way to the river. He paused to look at the sight before him.

'We are helping the gardener!' said the monkey king proudly. 'We checked the roots before watering to see how much each tree needed!'

The Bodhisatta stepped into the garden. He knelt beside a broken tree and touched its root gently.

'I know you wanted to help,' he said kindly. 'But good intentions without wisdom can sometimes do harm.'

The monkey king looked around at the mess they had made and sighed. 'We didn't mean to hurt them,' he said. 'We only wanted to do the job right.'

The Bodhisatta smiled. 'And now you've learnt something even more valuable. To help truly, you must first listen, learn and understand. That is the path of wisdom.'

From that day, the monkey king took a new vow to ask and learn before rushing to act. He taught his troop to do the same too.

The garden grew back in time. New saplings were planted. The monkeys still played and tumbled in the trees, though they never forgot the day they learnt that even kindness must walk hand-in-hand with wisdom.

2. THE LITTLE QUAIL AND THE BIG NET

In a quiet, green forest where ancient trees stretched towards the sky, a little quail was born. This quail was the Bodhisatta, who had chosen to be born as a small creature to help others and guide them to kindness and wisdom.

Among shadowy patches and golden sunlight, Bodhisatta grew up with a cheerful flock of quails. There were fifty of them, their brown feathers perfectly blending with the forest floor. Every morning, they would fly from branch to branch, chirping and singing as they poked around the forest for seeds. The younger birds would race each other to the feeding spots, while the elders shared stories of the seasons. The forest was their home, and life was peaceful.

But not all who entered the forest came in peace. One misty morning, a hunter crept among the trees. He carried a net so wide and fine that even the strongest wings could not break through it. But his cleverest weapon was not his net—it was his voice.

The hunter had learnt to imitate the call of a quail so

perfectly that it fooled even the cleverest of birds. Hiding behind a tree, he cupped his hands and gave the call. 'Pee-weet! Pee-weet!'

Hearing what sounded like a friendly call, the quails flew down. The hunter waited. Then, with a swift motion, he flung the net. And just like that, the quails found themselves trapped. Wings flapped. Beaks cried out. Feet scrambled. But the net held fast.

The hunter smiled, gathering the heavy bundle of birds, and slung it over his shoulder.

From a high branch, the Bodhisatta watched in silence. That evening, the Bodhisatta gathered the remaining flock around him. 'My friends,' he said, 'the hunter is one, but we are many. He catches us because we panic and act alone. But if we work together, we can outsmart him.'

The flock chirped and listened. 'The next time the net falls,' he continued, 'slip your head through the holes. Then, all at once, flap your wings with all your strength. If we rise together, we can lift the net into the air and carry it far away. When we reach the thorny hillside, drop the net there and walk away. The thorns will catch it, and the hunter will have to spend a whole day trying to get it out.'

The next morning, the hunter came and made the call again. The quails flew down. The net came flying. But this time, as soon as it landed, the birds remembered the plan. 'Now!' called the Bodhisatta. Heads pushed through the gaps. Wings beat and the net rose into the air. The quails flew together, flapping as one, and carried the net across the forest to the thorny hillside. There, they dropped it and flew away. When the hunter arrived, he found only his net, tangled and torn in the thorns.

THE LITTLE QUAIL AND THE BIG NET

He returned home empty-handed. 'Another empty day?' said his wife.

'They've learnt to lift the net,' the hunter grumbled. 'They escape every time. But it won't last. They'll start quarrelling. Birds always do.'

And he was right.

For many days, the birds flew together and escaped. But one morning, as they pecked at scattered seeds, a young quail accidentally stepped on another's foot.

'Ow! Watch where you're hopping!' snapped the second.

'It wasn't on purpose,' said the first. 'I didn't see you.'

Soon, they were quarrelling bitterly. Then the others joined in.

'He pushed me too yesterday!'

'She pecked at my wing for no reason!'

The Bodhisatta flew down between them. 'Friends,' he said, 'don't forget that it is our unity keeps us safe. If we quarrel, the net will trap us again.'

But the quails turned away. Bodhisatta saw that their pride had grown louder than their wisdom. Quietly, he gathered those who still listened and led them to another part of the forest.

The next morning, the hunter returned. But this time, the birds were too busy arguing to notice the net being thrown. Some flapped early, some flapped late. The net wobbled, but stayed on the ground. The hunter rushed forwards and gathered the birds with ease.

From a branch above, the Bodhisatta watched with sorrow. That evening, he spoke to the younger birds beside him. 'Even the heaviest net can be lifted by wings that beat as one. But when we quarrel, even the lightest thread can bind us.'

3. THE RAIN OF RICHES

Once the Bodhisatta lived as a student under Devadatta, a powerful brahmin priest who was known across kingdoms for his wisdom and knowledge of ancient magic.

This priest knew a secret spell passed down through generations. When the stars and planets aligned just right, once each year, he could chant the magic words and shower a rain of gold, silver, pearls and precious gems from the sky. The spell was dangerous, but the treasure it brought was dazzling.

One day, the priest and the Bodhisatta were travelling through a thick forest on their way to a temple far away. As they walked beneath the towering trees and winding vines, a band of robbers suddenly jumped out from behind the bushes. The rough men tied up the priest to a tree nearby, and pushed the Bodhisatta roughly to the ground. 'Go and fetch a ransom,' their leader growled. 'If you do not return by tomorrow's sunset, your master will not live to see another sunrise.'

Before he left, the Bodhisatta turned to his bound teacher and said quietly, 'Master, do not cast the spell tonight, even if the stars are perfect. It will end only in trouble.' The priest nodded, but in his heart, pride was already growing.

That night, as the robbers sat around their crackling fire, the priest sat quietly nearby. His mind raced with thoughts of escape. 'Why should I wait for my student?' he reasoned. 'These men will let me go if I give them treasure.' So he told the robbers about the spell. Their eyes grew wide with greed. Quickly, they untied him, gave him cool water and clean robes, and placed fragrant flowers on his shoulders.

As the stars slowly shifted into position, the priest stood beneath the sky in a small clearing. The robbers formed a circle around him. He raised his arms and chanted the spell. The air shimmered and grew thick. Then, with a loud whoosh, jewels began to fall from the sky like rain. Gold coins, Pearls, Rubies and diamonds sparkled like captured stars. The robbers gathered under the shade of a tree and whispered to each other. Now that the priest had joined them, they believed their luck had turned.

'With him on our side,' one of them said, 'we'll be rich beyond measure!' The others nodded, already dreaming of more gold and jewels. The robbers cheered, shouting with joy, filling their bags with more wealth than they had ever imagined.

But greed, once awakened, is never satisfied. Taking the treasure, they marched off with the priest. But before they reached the edge of the forest, another gang of robbers who had heard rumours of the magical treasure leapt out from the shadows. 'We've heard of your magic, priest,' their captain said, his sword drawn. 'Call down more treasure or you'll never leave this forest alive.' The priest shook his head wearily. 'The stars must be perfectly aligned. I need to wait a full year before I can cast the spell again.'

The new gang grew angry and killed him where he stood, splitting him into two with their sword. Then they turned on the first group, killed them all and stole the treasure. But greed filled their hearts like poison. They could not agree on how to divide it. One by one, they fought and murdered each other until there were only two of them. One stayed behind to guard the treasure and the other went to fetch rice from a nearby village. But greed had poisoned his heart completely. He laced the rice with poison, hoping to keep all the treasure for himself. When he returned, the first man struck him down fearing a trick. Then, hungry from the long wait, he sat and ate the rice.

He died with a full stomach and empty hands, the treasure glittering uselessly around him.

When the Bodhisatta returned with the ransom money three days later, he found nothing but the fallen bodies scattered around piles of treasure.

He sighed deeply and said 'Greed not only destroys the greedy, but also those around them. Wealth without wisdom is like fire without a hearth - it burns everything it touches.'

He gave all the treasure to the poor in the nearby villages and chose to live a life of peace, giving and wisdom.

4. THE TREE THAT WAS NOT A MANGO

Once, the Bodhisatta was born as a wise and kind merchant. He led caravans of oxcarts across deserts, forests and rocky mountain passes, trading silk, spices and precious stones with faraway lands. His journeys were long, but he always made sure his people and animals were safe. The merchants who travelled with him fully trusted him.

Once, his caravan entered a vast forest that stretched for many miles.

Before setting up camp in a small clearing, the Bodhisatta gathered his men around him. Their faces were weathered from months of travel. 'Listen carefully, my friends,' he said, his voice serious but gentle. 'This forest hides dangers that cannot be seen. Many trees look harmless, but some can kill with just one bite of their fruit. Do not eat anything you find growing here, no matter how familiar it may seem.'

The men nodded and began to unpack their supplies. Some cooked rice, others lit fires or fed the oxen. The Bodhisatta stayed behind for a while, helping another group of merchants whose carts had gotten stuck.

Meanwhile, a few of his men wandered deeper into the forest, drawn by curiosity. There, in a sunny spot, they discovered a magnificent tree with golden fruit hanging from its branches. The fruit looked exactly like mangoes.

'It's a mango tree!' one of them exclaimed. 'We've had nothing fresh in days.'

'Let's take just one each,' said another man. 'The master will understand.'

One of the men quickly stepped forwards. He grabbed hold of a low branch and began to climb, balancing carefully as he reached for the nearest golden fruit. Below, another man stood ready, arms outstretched.

'Careful!' he whispered. 'Toss it down gently.'

The man in the tree plucked a fruit and dropped it into his friend's waiting hands. One by one, they picked more. Soon, all of them were biting into the golden mangoes. The fruit was sweet and juicy, just as they had hoped

Just then, the Bodhisatta arrived and saw them by the tree.

'Stop!' he cried. His eyes were wide with worry.

He looked at the tree carefully, and then the half-eaten fruit in their hands. Suddenly their breath turned shallow, their faces went pale and their hands trembled. Without another word, he opened a small leather pouch he always carried and gave each man several drops of a bitter elixir made from rare herbs.

Slowly, their breathing eased. Their faces, which had begun to pale, grew warm. The trembling in their hands stopped.

'You are very lucky, my friends,' he said quietly, his voice filled with relief. 'This is not a mango tree. It is a kimpakka tree, one of the most dangerous plants in this forest. Its fruit looks exactly like a mango, but even one bite can be fatal.'

The men stared at the tree in horror, realising how close they had come to disaster.

In a nearby village hidden among the hills, people had been watching the forest road for days. They often waited for travellers to eat the kimpakka fruit. When people died, they would sneak into the forest at night and steal the wagons, oxen and valuable goods.

That morning, they expected to find lifeless bodies by the roadside. But instead, they saw a healthy camp, alive with laughter, and the sounds of men preparing for the next day's journey. The puzzled villagers approached the Bodhisatta, 'Master, how did you know the tree was not a real mango? Even those of us who live here sometimes cannot tell them apart.'

The Bodhisatta smiled gently and replied, 'If this were truly a mango tree, it would have been picked clean long ago by hungry travellers and merchants. But this tree was full of ripe fruit, untouched. That alone told me something was terribly wrong.'

The villagers were amazed at his wisdom and began to feel shame for their wicked plans. Some of them decided to stop stealing and find honest work instead.

Later, as the men rested around the flickering campfire, the Bodhisatta sat among them and said, 'Not everything that looks safe is safe, and not everything that appears familiar can be trusted. Sometimes, the greatest danger hides behind what seems most ordinary and harmless. So, we must use not only our eyes, but our minds, our experience and our careful observation.'

5. THE BRAVE PRINCE AND THE FOREST OGRE

Long ago, the Bodhisatta was born as a royal prince, the first son of a wise king. The day of his birth was one of great celebration. Drums were played, garlands were hung and trays of food were sent out to feed the poor.

The king summoned eight hundred brahmin priests to perform the naming and blessing ceremony. After studying the stars and ancient scriptures, they bowed to the king and queen and declared, 'This child is no ordinary boy. He will grow into a ruler of extraordinary courage, wisdom and compassion. He will protect the weak and give without hesitation.'

The prince grew into a strong and intelligent youth, skilled in battle and debate. But he was also kind to servants, helped those in need and listened to others without judgment. At sixteen, the king sent the Bodhisatta to the city of Taxila, to learn from the best teachers and schools.

In Taxila, the Bodhisatta studied history, weapon skills and the ways of ruling justly. His teacher was impressed by the prince's intelligence and humility. At the end of his studies,

THE BRAVE PRINCE AND THE FOREST OGRE

the teacher said to him, 'You have learnt all I can teach. As a gift, I give you these five special weapons. But remember, true strength does not lie in weapons, but in wisdom.'

With reverence, the Bodhisatta set off on the journey home.

His path led him to a dense forest in the mountains. Villagers along the way warned him, 'Do not enter that forest, noble prince. A fearsome ogre lives there. He feeds on all who pass through. Many brave men have gone in, but None have come out.'

But the Bodhisatta, said calmly. 'I do not fear death,' he said. 'Let me see what lies within.' With a calm heart and clear mind, he walked into the forest. The deeper he went, the forest grew quieter. Then suddenly, a deep growl echoed through the woods. From behind the trees emerged the gigantic ogre. Standing taller than a palm tree, he had thick fur with tangled roots and claws as long as daggers.

But the Bodhisatta did not run. With steady hands, he fired an arrow at the ogre. It struck the ogre, but only on its matted fur. He kept firing one after the other but none could pierce the beast's skin.

The ogre roared and rushed at him. The Bodhisatta threw his sword. It hit the ogre and fell to the ground. He swung his heavy club—it struck the ogre's side, but stuck fast in the fur. Still, he stood his ground.

'I will fight you with my bare hands if I must!' he cried. He struck the ogre with both fists, but even his limbs became trapped in the thick fur. The ogre grabbed him in a crushing grip, ready to eat him. But then, the ogre paused. Something was different. He looked into the prince's face and saw no panic,

no hatred and no plea for life. What he saw instead was courage and calm.

'You are not like the others,' the ogre said, puzzled. 'They screamed and begged. You do not. Why?'

The Bodhisatta spoke gently. 'Because I understand the nature of life. I'm not afraid to let go. I know what we do have consequences. Your life of cruelty is a result of choices made long ago. But if you wish to change, you can end this path of pain.'

The ogre fell silent. He had never heard such words. He said at last, 'I am tired of being a monster. I no longer want this life.'

'Then start now,' said the Bodhisatta. 'Release your anger and Choose to be kind. You can still change your fate'

With tears in his eyes, the ogre gently set the prince down. His heart felt light.

The Bodhisatta bowed to him and walked out of the forest unharmed, his mind at peace.

He was welcomed back to the kingdom with songs and cheers. Years later, he became king and ruled with fairness and wisdom. His fame spread far and wide.

And deep in the forest, the ogre kept his promise. He never harmed another creature again. The forest became a place of quiet and peace once more.

6. THE FOOLISH PRICE MAKER

Once the Bodhisatta was born as a wise and honest man, serving as the royal price maker to the king of Benares. The king loved wealth more than wisdom, and gold more than fairness. He wore fine robes and sat on a jewelled throne, but his heart was always thinking of coins and counting his treasures.

'More gold!' he would cry, looking at his chests of coins. The Bodhisatta, calm and fair-minded, had been chosen to set prices for all the palace's trade. Whether it was elephants or emeralds, spices or silks, he judged every deal honestly. He always stood for what was right, and was trusted and respected by all. But the king grew impatient. He watched the market stalls from his balcony and scowled at the careful records the Bodhisatta kept.

'He's too fair,' the king muttered one morning. 'Always thinking of the people. But what about me? Why shouldn't I be richer?'

Just then, while walking through the city streets, the king spotted a young fruit seller at the market. The boy had a wide grin, a quick tongue, and a knack for selling mangoes. 'Hmm,' thought the king. 'This fellow is clever, eager to please and knew how to win people over. He'll surely bring me more gold.'

And so, without warning or farewell, the king dismissed the Bodhisatta and made the fruit seller his new price maker. The young man was thrilled. He marched into the palace, puffed with pride, and set to work. He cut down the prices the palace paid, hardly giving anything at all to hard-working traders. At the same time, he raised what the palace charged, until no one could afford a thing.

The treasure room began to swell with coins. The king was delighted. But outside the palace, the city started to waste away. The markets grew silent and Fewer people came to trade. The cheerful buzz of Benares was replaced by cold eyes and quiet anger.

Then, one morning, a wealthy merchant arrived at the city leading a line of strong, shining horses–five hundred in all. Each horse had been trained with care, their coats brushed until they gleamed in the sun. He hoped to sell them to the palace.

The new price maker met him outside the stables. He quoted a price after giving the horses one lazy glance. 'One cup of rice. That's what they're worth.' He spoke.

'Pardon me?' the merchant asked in disbelief, 'one cup of rice ... for five hundred royal horses?' The price maker only grinned.

The merchant said nothing. He bowed stiffly, turned to walk away and went straight to the home of the Bodhisatta.

The Bodhisatta calmly listened to the merchant. Having heard the story, he offered the merchant a solution, 'Go back to the price maker and lure him with a gift. Then ask him to explain what a cup of rice is truly worth in the presence

THE FOOLISH PRICE MAKER

of the king. Let him say it clearly, in the royal court.' The merchant nodded.

The next morning, the palace was full of nobles and ministers. The king sat high on his throne. The merchant stepped forwards and bowed down to the king.

'Your Majesty,' he said, 'your price maker has made a wise judgement, and I am truly grateful. But I am a simple man, and I do not understand the value of things. May I ask him to kindly explain the true worth of one cup of rice?'

The young minister puffed out his chest, and started to speak, 'One cup of rice is worth the entire city of Benares. The palace, the people, the royal gardens and even the throne itself. That is the price!'

For a moment, the hall was silent.

Then the entire court started to chuckle, growing into a roaring laughter.

The king's face turned red. He realised, in an instant, what a fool had been. He had entrusted such a high position on a clueless person.

'Enough!' he shouted. He turned to the merchant. 'You shall be paid fairly, as your horses deserve.' Then he sent for the Bodhisatta, and restored him to his rightful place.

From that day on, the king no longer judged people by their smiles or fast talk. He learnt to trust those who had proved their worth through thought and fairness.

And the Bodhisatta continued to serve with honesty, never seeking riches, but always bringing balance and peace. He knew that even kings must choose their advisors wisely. Because when a fool sits on a high seat, the kingdom feels the fall.

7. THE TALE OF AVISHYA THE UNSHAKEN

Long ago, in a bustling city filled with traders and temples, the Bodhisatta was born into a wealthy family of respected merchants. In that life, he was known as Avishya, which means the invincible one.

As he grew, Avishya showed a calm mind and a kind heart. He studied the sacred texts, treated all people with fairness and helped anyone in need. When he became the head of his guild, he gained great riches. But his joy never came from gold or jewels. It came from caring for the poor and needy.

Every morning, he welcomed a stream of visitors to his home. He treated the beggars and travellers who came to his door with a wholesome meal. Avishya offered robes, food and rest without hesitation. He never kept count and never turned anyone away. He found joy in seeing the smiles of those around him.

In the heavens above, Indra, king of the gods, heard of this generous merchant.

THE TALE OF AVISHYA THE UNSHAKEN

'A man so wealthy, yet holds on to nothing?' he said. 'Let us see how far his kindness truly goes.'

So Indra set out to test Avishya. One by one, all of Avishya's treasures vanished. His coins were gone. His fine beds and silks disappeared. His grand house crumbled. At last, all he had left was a sickle and a rope.

But Avishya did not sigh or shed a single tear. He tied the rope around his waist, picked up the sickle and walked to the fields outside the city. The sun blazed overhead. The earth was cracked and dry beneath his feet. His hands became sore, but still he worked, cutting the grass with care. He carried the bundles to the market and sold them for a few small coins.

With that little money, he bought food and gave it to the poor. He bought cloth and offered it to monks. He ate nothing himself. Yet his eyes stayed peaceful and his smile remained.

Indra watched from the clouds and could hardly believe it.

'Even now he gives? Even in hunger and poverty?'

To test him further, Indra took the form of a glowing being. He came down from the sky, and stood before the tired and starving Avishya. He squinted his eyes, blinded by the shining form of Indra.

'Avishya,' he said, 'you were once rich and powerful. Now look at you. You should use your earnings to build a new house, to feed yourself first. You cannot give forever.'

Avishya placed his bundle of grass on the ground and looked up at the shining figure.

'Wise one,' he said softly, 'wealth may come one day and vanish the next'. But when I give, even a single grain of rice, I feel joy that no gold can match. This is the life I choose, and I will not turn away from it.'

Indra gazed at him for a long moment. Then a smile spread across his face.

'You have shown the truth of your heart,' he said. 'You give to those around you, not for praise, but from a deep wish to help.'

At once, the sky opened and warm light flooded the earth. Avishya's home was restored, more beautiful than before. The rooms were filled with grain and fruit. The gardens bloomed with mangoes and marigolds. His neighbours came running, amazed by the sudden change.

But Avishya remained the same. Whether in wealth or in poverty, he greeted each guest with the same kindness. And so, his story passed from village to village and from one age to the next, not because of what he owned, but because he never stopped giving, even when he had nothing left but the strength of his own hands and the goodness of his heart.

8. THE CLEVER CROW

Once the Bodhisatta was born as a crow. He lived by a river that flowed through a wide green valley. On either side of the river, tall trees rose into the sky, their branches full of rustling leaves. A great flock of crows lived in the heights of the trees. One among them was the Bodhisatta, known for his sharp eyes, quiet nature and calm advice. He did not chatter or boast like the other birds. When he spoke, the others listened.

On sunny days, the flock of crows would rise with the first light. They pecked at scattered grains, fallen fruit and the odd scrap left behind by farmers. Calling to one another as they flew, they scoured the fields in noisy, cheerful groups

One bright morning, the sky was clear, and the breeze carried the promise of a warm day. A group of young crows flew out early, calling to one another as they soared over the meadows.

'Let's search near the wheat fields today!' called one.

'I heard the farmers left grain after harvesting,' said another.

They flew in high loops and dipped low over the trees, laughing and racing each other in the wind.

Soon, they spotted something in the grass below. In the middle of a sunlit clearing was a shining heap of grain—golden and fresh, spread in a perfect circle.

The young crows gasped and slowed their wings.

'Look at that!' said one. 'All that grain—and no one in sight!'

'It must be our lucky day,' said another. 'No farmer, no scarecrow, nothing!'

'Let's eat before someone else finds it!' cried a third, already beginning to swoop down.

But just then, the Bodhisatta landed silently on a branch nearby. He had followed them from a distance, as he often did.

'Wait,' he said. The young crows flapped their wings and turned towards him.

'What is it?' asked one. 'There's no danger. Can't you smell it? It's fresh!'

'Yes,' said another. 'Why stop now?'

The Bodhisatta looked carefully at the pile of grain. His keen eyes narrowed.

'Look more closely,' he said. 'Does it not seem strange? Who leaves a perfect pile of grain in the middle of a field, far from any barn or cart? This is no accident.'

The young crows looked again, but all they saw was the golden food gleaming in the sun.

'I don't see anything,' said one, frowning.

'There,' said the Bodhisatta, pointing with one wingtip. 'Do you see that fine thread? It's almost invisible, but it runs through the grain like a spider's web.'

The crows squinted. Now, just barely, they could make it out—thin strands of thread connecting the grains like beads on a string.

'And there,' the Bodhisatta continued, his voice calm, 'in the bushes—something metal glinting. A net. A trap. And behind it, a hunter waiting.'

The young crows shivered. One of them gave a low whistle.

'I didn't see any of that,' he whispered.

'We would've flown straight into it,' said another.

'Yes,' said the Bodhisatta. 'And you would not have flown out again. This is how hunters work. They make what is dangerous look like a gift. They use greed to blind you.'

The crows rose from the branches and flew back to a safer tree by the riverbank. From there, they watched the field. When he saw that the crows were not coming that day, the hunter stood up from the bushes, disappointed. He gathered his net and walked away empty-handed.

That evening, the crows returned to their favourite tree by the water's edge. As the sun went down, they thought about everything that happened that day.

'I feel foolish,' said one of the young crows. 'I almost dove straight in.'

'It's not foolish to be hungry,' said the Bodhisatta gently. 'But it is dangerous to trust anything that seems too easy. Even a pile of grain can hide a trap. Look with your eyes—but also with your mind.' A third young crow nodded. 'From now on, I'll think first. Even when food is right in front of me.' And from that day on, the flock was more careful. They looked twice. They asked questions.

Even a simple crow can be clever—if he watches, waits and thinks.

9. THE DEER WHO PLAYED DEAD

Once the Bodhisatta was born as a deer. He lived deep in a quiet forest, where tall trees reached for the sky and the air was filled with birdsongs. The Bodhisatta was strong, calm and wise, and he led a large herd of deer who trusted him completely.

Among the herd was his younger sister. One day, she came to visit the Bodhisatta with her young son—a bright-eyed fawn with a quick step and an eager heart.

She bowed her head and said, 'Dear brother, my son is growing up fast. He can run well, but he is still new to the ways of the forest. I fear for him when the hunters come. Will you teach him how to survive?'

The Bodhisatta looked at the young deer, who stood tall and alert beside his mother.

'Yes,' he said. 'Bring him to me tomorrow at sunrise. I will teach him all that he must know.'

The next morning, as the first light touched the treetops, the young deer arrived. He followed the Bodhisatta closely, listening carefully.

THE DEER WHO PLAYED DEAD

'Watch the ground before you step,' said the Bodhisatta one day. 'Hunters dig pits and lay snares that are hard to see.'

Another day, he warned, 'If you smell fire or hear strange sounds, do not run without thinking. Stop and listen. Let your ears guide your feet.'

The Bodhisatta taught not only how to avoid danger, but how to stay calm when it came. 'Fear makes the feet move faster,' he said, 'but wisdom tells them where to go.' He showed the young deer how to read broken twigs, to smell smoke carried by the wind, and to tell the difference between the sound of falling fruit and a hunter's step. The young deer listened closely, asked questions and never gave up.

Day by day, the young deer learnt how to move quietly, how to blend into the shadows, and how to stay calm in times of fear. He never missed a lesson and practised everything he was taught.

Then, soon after the lessons were done, the young deer came of age and began to wander out alone. The morning was warm, and the forest peaceful. Birds chirped, and a breeze stirred the leaves. The deer stepped carefully through the undergrowth, alert but at ease.

Suddenly, out of nowhere, a snare hidden beneath the grass tightened around his leg. He was trapped.

He froze for a moment, his heart pounding. He kicked and twisted, trying to shake it loose, but the snare only pulled tighter. But then calmly tried to remember his lessons. Instead of struggling, he lay down gently. He stretched out his legs, turned his eyes upward and let his tongue hang out of his mouth. He slowed his breath until it barely moved his chest. Flies began to buzz around him, and crows gathered in the nearby trees, thinking he was already dead.

Sometime later, the hunter returned. He stepped out of the trees and looked at the deer carefully.

'it's caught a dead one,' he muttered. 'And already rotting. Useless.'

He loosened the rope and went off to find wood to make a fire.

As soon as the rope slipped free, the young deer leapt to his feet and ran like the wind. He did not stop until he reached the safety of the herd.

His mother was waiting, her eyes full of worry.

'My son!' she cried. 'Are you hurt?'

'I was caught in a trap,' he said, breathing hard. 'But I remembered uncle's lessons. I lay still and pretended to be dead. The hunter believed it and let me go. That's how I escaped.'

His mother ran to the Bodhisatta and told him everything.

The wise deer listened quietly and nodded. 'He has learnt well. In times of danger, it is the mind—not speed or strength—that saves us.'

From that day on, the tale of the clever young deer was told again and again. The fawns listened closely, and even the older deer repeated the story with respect. They had all learnt a truth that would stay with them:

Bravery is good. Strength is useful. But wisdom can save your life.

10. THE LOTUS ROOTS

Once, in a quiet land surrounded by forests and lakes, the Bodhisatta was born as the eldest son into a wealthy and respected family. But he was not interested in any of his father's wealth. As he grew older, his parents began searching for a suitable bride. 'It is time you were married,' they told him gently. 'A good home, a good wife—these are the things that bring happiness.' But the young man only smiled and shook his head. 'I have no wish to be tied to the world,' he said quietly. 'I seek a different path.'

His parents tried many times to change his mind, but his heart was calm and firm. He wished for nothing more than a life of peace and wisdom. As time went on, his parents grew old and eventually passed away. After that, he chose to live a simple, ascetic life in the forest. He was followed by his six brothers. They took great care to make sure they took only what they needed, to keep their promise of living alone even when leaving their homes. Along with their younger sister and two faithful servants, they travelled until they found a quiet spot by

a calm lake. They made up their minds to live near its calm and clear waters lined by the cool shade of trees.

There, the brothers built small huts made from palm leaves and soft branches. Each hut was simple but strong enough to keep out the rain and stay cool in the sun. The air smelled fresh and was full of damp earth and wildflowers. Birds sang sweet songs in the morning and the soft rustle of leaves filled the quiet forest.

Each brother stayed in his own hut to meditate. They spoke to no one except on the fifth day when they gathered near the lake to listen to the teachings of the Bodhisatta. He was calm and wise and his teachings spoke of kindness, patience and the joy of simple living. Even in silence his presence brought peace to all.

They ate only the roots of the lotus plants that grew in the lake. Every morning the two servants would quietly wade into the cool water feeling the soft mud beneath their feet. They pulled the long thick lotus roots from the lake bed and washed them clean in the clear water. Then they carefully placed the roots on large green lotus leaves, each leaf shining like a small plate under the bright sunlight.

High above in the heavens, Indra, the king of the gods watched the family from his heavenly palace. He admired their calm and devotion but wondered if their hearts were truly free from anger, fear or hunger. He thought 'Are they really as patient and kind as they seem?'

To find out, Indra decided to test them. Every day he secretly took the Bodhisatta's portion of lotus roots before the brothers could eat. The Bodhisatta found nothing waiting for him but he did not show anger or sadness. Instead, he remained peaceful and silent.

THE LOTUS ROOTS

Days passed and the Bodhisatta grew very thin. His cheeks were sunken and his eyes looked tired but still gentle. When the fifth day came and the brothers met by the lake, they noticed their eldest brother's weakened body and quiet voice.

Instead of becoming angry or upset one brother spoke softly, 'Whoever has taken the roots is in need of kindness. Let us pray for them to find peace.'

The other brothers joined in. They closed their eyes and whispered prayers full of hope and forgiveness. The sister and servants did the same. No one blamed or scolded. Even the Bodhisatta smiled gently and said a prayer for the one who had taken the food.

Indra was deeply moved by their kindness. He appeared in front of the brothers in the form of a shiny light.

'I am the one who took your lotus roots,' Indra said. 'I wished to test your hearts and see if your kindness was true. You have passed my test. Your patience and love are pure.'

But the Bodhisatta looked at Indra calmly and said 'We do not give kindness for praise or reward. Our kindness comes from within from understanding that everyone needs care. Whether the gods watches or not our hearts stay gentle.'

Indra smiled warmly and bowed before the Bodhisatta. Then as softly as he had appeared, he vanished.

11. THE BRAVE LITTLE PARROT

In the heart of a wide green forest, the Bodhisatta was once born as a parrot. She looked plain, with no bright colours or decoration. Her feathers were plain, soft grey. But she was cheerful and kind, always ready to help others. She spoke gently to the old animals, played with the young ones and was friendly with everyone—deer, monkeys, squirrels and even the shy porcupines. Whenever someone was in trouble, the little parrot was the first to come to their help.

One hot afternoon, the air turned dry and sharp. The breeze stopped. A stillness fell over the forest. Then, with a crack loud as thunder, lightning struck a tree. In seconds, flames burst through the leaves and spread fast.

The fire raced from one tree to the next. Squirrels dashed from hollow trunks. Snakes slid through grass. Birds took flight. The Bodhisatta saw smoke curling into the sky and cried out as loud as she could, 'Fire! Fire! Run to the river!'

She flew above the flames, guiding animals through the smoke. Many made it to the river's edge, where they stood trembling, their eyes wide.

'We are safe now,' said the deer.

'There is nothing more to be done,' said the boar.

But the Bodhisatta looked back. She soared high into the sky to get a better view of the forest. Flames had trapped many animals still deep in the woods. She heard the cries of birds and beasts echoed through the forest.

She could not sit by the water while others were left behind.

'I saw a way through the fire,' she said. 'I have to try.'

The animals gathered at the edge of the forest tried to stop her.

'You'll get burnt!' warned the elephant. 'What can a bird do against a fire like that?'

'You did what you could,' Said the old monkey. 'Let the fire pass little one!'

But without listening to their warnings, she flew to the riverbank, dipped her body in the water and soaked her feathers. She found a wide leaf, filled it with water and lifted it in her claws. Then she flew back into the forest, dropping the water over a patch of flame.

It hissed and vanished. The fire flared again. She flew back, filled the leaf with water and dropped it over the flames. Again, and again. Her feathers turned black with soot. Her beak cracked and her wings trembled.

Animals at the river watched in silence. Some shook their heads. Some looked away. But the little parrot did not stop.

High above, Indra watched from the sky. His golden eyes followed her tiny shape through the smoke. Other gods saw her too.

'Foolish bird,' they said. 'She cannot stop a fire.'

But Indra saw more than just a bird. He saw her courage and unwillingness to give up. His heart grew heavy. He changed into a mighty eagle and swept down from the clouds.

He found her flapping weakly over the fire.

'Little one,' he said, 'you have done enough. Come away now. The fire is too strong.'

But the Bodhisatta looked up, eyes red and full of tears. 'If I turn away, who will help them?'

Indra flew beside her. 'But look at you—your wings are burnt, your feathers are torn. You are small. You cannot put out this fire alone.'

She turned her head, eyes full of soot and tears. 'Maybe I can't,' she said softly, 'but doing nothing would be worse. I have to try. Even a little water might help someone escape.'

Indra was silent. The smoke curled around them. The little parrot flew on.

Suddenly, tears started to well up in Indra's eyes. They fell, drop by drop, on to the raging fire below. The flames hissed, sank and faded. The smoke cleared. The sky turned blue again. One last tear landed on the little parrot. It cooled her burnt feathers.

The Bodhisatta looked out at her forest, healed and alive. And that is how the forest came to know that bravery is not about size or strength, but about choosing to care for others in times of need.

12. THE PARTRIDGE WHO PLANTED A TREE

In a peaceful valley near the snowy peaks of the Himalayas, a grand old banyan tree stood tall. Among its branches and winding roots lived many birds, squirrels and other small creatures. It was also home to three unlikely friends: a monkey, an elephant and a partridge. But the partridge was no ordinary bird. He was the Bodhisatta, born with great wisdom and kindness.

At first, they lived together in harmony. But as time passed, each began to think they knew best. The monkey leapt about giving orders. The elephant stomped around choosing paths on his own. The partridge chirped his thoughts and then flew off without waiting. Decisions became arguments, and arguments became habits.

'We should build our shelter near the big rock,' said the elephant firmly.

'Too hot!' snapped the monkey. 'You only like it because you like sitting in the sun all day!'

'And you only want to stay near trees so you can swing around and show off,' the elephant grumbled.

The partridge fluttered down. 'You two never listen. I found a better place by the stream, but I suppose you'll argue about that too!' 'Because you fly off before we've even finished talking!' said the monkey. 'And who asked you to decide for everyone?' huffed the elephant.

Soon, even the smallest tasks turned into squabbles, and the forest no longer felt like a peaceful home.

The wise partridge started to fear for their sacred friendship. If they kept arguing with one another, it would turn to bitter quarrels very soon, and then bring an end to their friendship. He decided that this should no longer be allowed to happen. One afternoon, the partridge gathered his friends beneath the banyan tree.

'We have been friends for a long time,' he said, 'but we often quarrel like strangers. I believe we need someone to guide us. Perhaps the one who is oldest among us should lead.'

The monkey scratched his head. 'That seems fair.'

The elephant gave a slow nod. 'Let us see who has known this tree the longest. That one shall guide the rest.'

The elephant began. 'When I was young and still learning to use my trunk, this tree was only a small bush. I could step right over it. Its tallest leaves just brushed my belly.'

The monkey then spoke. 'When I was little, I could sit on the ground and still reach the topmost leaves with my paws. So, I knew it when it was barely the size of a shrub.'

Then it was the partridge's turn. He looked up at the tree, and his eyes softened.

'I remember a time before this tree even grew. I once lived near another tree, far from here. It dropped many seeds. I ate one of those seeds and flew over this very spot. I left the seed here in the earth. That is how this tree was born. I knew it before it was born.'

The monkey's eyes widened. The elephant let out a thoughtful breath.

'Then you are the oldest among us,' said the monkey.

'And the wisest,' added the elephant.

From that day forwards, his friends listened to his counsel. The Bodhisatta guided them with gentle words and clear thinking. He taught them to speak with care, to live with respect and to share what they had.

The monkey stopped shouting. The elephant began to listen more closely. And together they kept peace in their corner of the forest.

They no longer argued about who was right or strongest. They only asked what was kind, what was wise and what was fair.

And so, under the spreading branches of the tree the Bodhisatta had once planted, the three friends lived in harmony. With hearts full of respect, they each followed the path of goodness.

And so they learnt—with age comes wisdom, and with wisdom comes peace.

13. THE JACKAL AND THE RAT KING

In the deep shade of an ancient forest lived a mighty rat. He was not like other rats. This was the Bodhisatta, who ruled over hundreds of rats in the forest. He was strong and as big as a young boar. He lead the rats with wisdom and compassion, and had their complete trust.

They lived in a safe corner of the forest, under a burrow where they hid themselves from the dangers of the wild.

Not far from their home roamed a jackal with a cunning mind and a belly that growled with hunger. One day, the jackal came upon the trail of the rats on their way back home. When he saw how many of them there were, he licked his lips and began to think.

'I cannot chase so many,' he thought. 'But if I appear wise and holy, perhaps they will trust me.'

The jackal came up with a mischievous plan. The next day, the jackal stood still near their burrow. He faced the sun, stood on one leg and held his mouth wide open. Then he closed his eyes, looking as if he was thinking quietly and deeply to himself.

THE JACKAL AND THE RAT KING

When the Bodhisatta passed by, leading his rats, he saw the jackal and stopped. The sight puzzled him. He had never seen such a pose before.

'What sort of being are you?' the Bodhisatta asked politely.

'I am called 'Godly',' said the jackal, without moving.

'Why do you stand on one leg?' asked the Bodhisatta. 'If I stood on all four, the earth would not bear my weight,' the jackal replied.

'And why is your mouth open?'

'I feed only on air,' said the jackal. 'It is pure and holy.' He started to feel sure that the rats would believe anything he says.

'And why do you face the sun?'

'To worship the great light that gives life to all,' he said.

The Bodhisatta bowed. 'Such holiness is rare. We will pay our respects to you from now on.'

From that day on, the rats came each morning and evening to honour the jackal. They believed he was a saintly creature. But each time they came and left, the jackal snatched the last rat in line and swallowed it whole. Then he wiped his mouth and stood once again like a statue. 'What an easy meal,' he murmured to himself. 'Let them keep bowing. I'll keep feasting.'

The rats did not notice at first. But in time, their numbers began to shrink. Gaps appeared in their lines. Mothers searched for sons, and brothers looked for brothers.

'Why are so many of us missing?' they asked the Bodhisatta.

He frowned and thought hard. He did not yet know the truth, but he began to suspect the jackal.

The next day, he told the others to walk ahead and said he would come last. As the rats passed the jackal, the Bodhisatta

hung back quietly. Just as he neared the edge of the clearing, the jackal leapt.

With sharp teeth bared and claws ready, he sprang at the Bodhisatta.

But the Bodhisatta was ready. He spun around and leapt at the jackal's throat and bit deep. Writhing and moaning in pain, the jackal breathed his last.

Hearing the loud cry, the rats came running back to the clearing. There lay the jackal, lifeless on the ground, and beside him stood the Bodhisatta, his grey fur ruffled and his breath still heavy from the fight. A gasp ran through the crowd. Some stared wide-eyed. Others looked from the jackal's sharp teeth to the scratches on the Bodhisatta's side.

'It was him all along,' one whispered. 'He fooled us,' another said bitterly.

The rats huddled close, stunned by what they had escaped. The Bodhisatta warned them that where people pretend to be holy just to deceive the honest and kind, there is really a heart full of betrayal. There is no true goodness in such false saints.

After that, the rats lived safely once more. No longer fooled by smooth words and empty poses, they followed the Bodhisatta's wise path with greater care.

14. THE JACKAL WHO TRIED TO ROAR

High up in the misty slopes of the Himalayas, golden light touched the rocks near a cave known as Gold Den. Here lived a mighty lion, who was strong and noble. This lion was the Bodhisatta, and the king of all beasts of the forest.

One morning, he set out from his den looking for food. He moved quietly through the forest, pacing each paw with care so as not to make a sound. Hiding behind the bushes, he saw a giant buffalo grazing through the plains. He started to make his moves carefully, and when the time was right, he pounced on the buffalo, biting on its neck and bringing it down. After he had his fill, he went to the lake to drink some cool water.

As he padded home with a full belly, a jackal stepped into his path. The jackal was thin and trembling with hunger. He dropped to the ground at the lion's feet.

'What do you want?' asked the lion, his voice deep and steady.

'Great one,' said the jackal, 'please let me be your servant. I will follow you faithfully.'

The Bodhisatta gave a small nod. 'If you serve me well, you may share my meals.'

From that day on, the jackal followed the lion and fed on what the lion left behind. He started to grow healthy and plump. He lived well and slept soundly in the safety of Gold Den.

One day, as the lion rested, he said to the jackal, 'Climb to the mountain top and watch the valleys. If you see any buffaloes, horses or elephants, tell me. Say, "Shine forth in thy might, Lord" and I shall hunt.'

The jackal did just that. He called to the lion, bowed low and said, 'Shine forth in thy might, Lord.' Then they set out together. The jackal led the way, his nose to the ground, sniffing for signs. Soon, he caught the scent of a herd of deer resting in a grassy clearing.

'This way, mighty one!' he whispered. 'A fine meal waits beyond the trees.'

The lion crouched low and crept forwards through the tall grass. The deer had no idea he was near. With a thunderous roar, the lion leapt out. The deer scattered in fear, but a slow old one couldn't escape. The lion brought it down in a single pounce.

When the hunt was over, the lion dragged the prey under a shady tree and began to eat. The jackal waited patiently at a distance, pretending to admire the lion's strength.

Only when the lion stepped away, belly full and ready for a nap, did the jackal sneak in. He licked his lips, picked over the bones and munched on whatever was left.

Afterwards, he curled up in the sun, tail flicking lazily and smiled to himself. 'What a fine life,' he murmured. 'Let the lion do all the work—I'll enjoy the feast.'

THE JACKAL WHO TRIED TO ROAR

As time passed, the jackal grew proud. One afternoon, after eating his fill, he looked at his four legs and thought, 'I have strong limbs too. Why should I depend on another's strength? I shall hunt for myself. And then I will get the lion to call me Lord.'

So the jackal went to the lion and said boldly, 'Let me rest in your cave today. You climb the mountain and tell me when you see an elephant. Then say, "Shine forth in thy might, jackal" and I shall do the rest.'

The lion gave him a long, serious look. 'Only lions can bring down elephants. No jackal has ever done such a thing. Be content with what you have.'

But the jackal would not give up. Again and again he asked, until the lion finally agreed.

That day, the jackal stretched out in the lion's place. The Bodhisatta climbed to the top of the hill. He saw a mighty elephant, thick with mud and in a restless mood. He returned to the den and said, 'Shine forth in thy might, jackal.'

Excited, the jackal leapt out and howled three times, looking around wildly. Without thinking, he ran straight at the elephant, aiming for its head. But he missed and landed at its feet.

The elephant trumpeted loudly and lifted one massive foot, crushing the jackal right there. His body was flattened, and then the elephant tossed him aside and disappeared into the forest.

The lion watched from above and sighed deeply. The Bodhisatta returned to his den and lived out his days in peace. He reminded himself that pride can make one forget their true place and that overestimating oneself can lead to a painful fall.

15. THE BOY WHO BROUGHT BACK A TIGER

Once, Bodhisatta was born as a wise and renowned teacher in the ancient city of Benares. He was born into a wealthy brahmin family, surrounded by comforts. But he gave up his riches, setting up a school to share his wisdom with others.

Every day, students came from far and wide to study with him. They sat under tall mango trees, listened to his calm voice and learnt about the world. Among his students was a clever boy named Sanjiva. Sanjiva was bright but also proud. He often wanted to show others how clever he was.

One day, the Bodhisatta taught Sanjiva a special spell. one that could bring the dead back to life. As they sat under a large banyan tree, the Bodhisatta spoke calmly.

'This is no ordinary chant, Sanjiva,' he said 'If spoken correctly, it can wake even those who have passed away.'

Sanjiva's eyes lit up. 'You mean ... I could bring anything back to life?'

'Yes,' said the Bodhisatta. 'But remember, this power is not a toy. It must be used with care and wisdom.'

'Of course, teacher,' Sanjiva replied quickly. 'I'll be careful. I promise.'

But he did not teach him the counter-charm, the spell that could stop or control what was raised. The Bodhisatta saw that Sanjiva was not yet wise enough to use such great power safely.

Not long after, Sanjiva went into the forest with a few of his classmates to gather firewood. As they wandered through the trees, they came across a dead tiger lying near a path. Sanjiva's eyes lit up. He turned to his friends and said, 'You know something? Master taught me a spell. A real one.'

'What kind of spell?' asked one of the boys, stepping back from the tiger.

'A spell that can bring the dead back to life,' Sanjiva said proudly. 'Anything. Even this tiger.'

The others stared at him. 'You're joking,' said one. 'No one can do that,' said another.

'Well, I can,' Sanjiva replied, raising his chin. You would believe it when I show it to you.

'You should not,' warned one of the boys. 'We do not know what might happen.'

But he was too blinded by his pride to listen to reason. The others quickly climbed up a tree nearby, afraid of what was coming. Sanjiva stood near the tiger, spoke the spell aloud and tapped it with a broken piece of pottery.

For a moment, nothing happened. Then, with a loud gasp, the tiger opened its eyes. It roared, shook its head and sprang up. It was hungry and wild, and it saw Sanjiva as easy prey. Before the boy could speak another word, the tiger leapt at him. With one terrible bite, it ended Sanjiva's life. Then, as quickly as it had come to life, the tiger fell down dead again.

The students watched in horror from the tree. When it was

safe, they climbed down and carried their friend's body back to their teacher.

The Bodhisatta listened carefully as they told him what had happened. He nodded slowly and looked into the eyes of each student.

'My dear children,' he said softly, 'what we learn is powerful. But power without wisdom is dangerous. Sanjiva used magic, but he did not understand the risk. He was warned, but he let pride lead the way.'

The students sat in silence, some quietly wiping tears for their lost friend. The Bodhisatta's voice was calm but carried a strong message. He told them that giving power to someone unkind or careless could bring trouble not only to that person, but also to everyone around them.

He spoke of Sanjiva, who had raised a fierce tiger only to be devoured by it. This showed how those who lift up danger without thinking carefully often face great harm themselves.

16. THE PET ELEPHANT

Long ago, when King Brahmadatta ruled the great city of Benares, there lived a special man called the Bodhisatta. He was born into a family of Brahmins, known far and wide for their wisdom and kindness. From a very young age, the Bodhisatta felt a deep call inside him. He wanted to learn more about life and help others. So, he left behind the comforts of his home and chose a quiet, simple life in the forests of the Himalayas.

There, in the woods, he became the leader of five hundred monks, people who lived peacefully and studied the ways of kindness and wisdom.

Among these monks lived a man named Indasamanagotta. He was a kind but stubborn man who did not like to listen to advice. He cared very much for a young elephant he once found in the forest. The elephant had lost its mother and was all alone in the wild. Indasamanagotta took the little elephant in and raised it with love and care. He gave it fruits to eat and talked to it in a cheerful voice. He made a little shelter for it near the monastery and took it down to the river for a bath every day. He fed it soft bananas, splashed water behind its ears and told it funny stories. The elephant grew happy and playful. It followed him around like a puppy, never wanting to be apart from him.

One day, the Bodhisatta heard about the elephant and the man who cared for it. He sent for Indasamanagotta to come to him. When the man arrived, the Bodhisatta looked at him kindly and asked, 'I have heard that you have a young elephant with you. Is this true?'

Indasamanagotta smiled and said, 'Yes, Teacher. The elephant is like a child to me.'

The Bodhisatta thought carefully and said, 'Elephants grow strong and wild. When they become big, they may forget the kindness they once knew. They can even become dangerous to those who cared for them. I think you should let the elephant go back to the forest.'

But Indasamanagotta shook his head. 'I cannot live without him,' he said firmly. 'He is my companion and my comfort.'

The Bodhisatta's voice grew soft but serious. 'If you do not let him go, you may come to regret it.'

Indasamanagotta did not listen. He kept caring for the elephant as it grew bigger and stronger. The elephant's steps shook the ground. His tusks grew to be thick and long, curling upwards like a horn.

One afternoon, the group of monks went deep into the forest to gather food. They left their small huts empty for a few days. But the elephant, left alone, felt something change inside him. A wild energy grew. His mind became filled with strange, dark thoughts.

'This hut feels like a cage. I'm not a dog or a cat—I'm an elephant! I will not be treated like a pet,' He said to himself. 'I will destroy everything inside. I will break the water jar, knock over the stone bench and tear up the roof. I will end the life of the hermit who locked me up. Then I will be free.'

Indasamanagotta was the first to come back, carrying the food he prepared for his pet. He was happy and hopeful as he walked towards the hut, not knowing what danger was near.

Suddenly, the elephant rushed out of the trees. He quickly grabbed Indasamanagotta with his strong trunk and threw him down. The man's head hit the ground hard, and he died instantly. The elephant let out a loud trumpet and disappeared into the deep forest.

When the other monks returned, they found the terrible scene. They hurried to tell the Bodhisatta what had happened.

The Bodhisatta listened quietly and then spoke, 'This sad event shows the danger of holding tightly to those who are stubborn and unkind. We must be careful about the company we keep because it shapes our lives.'

17. THE OWL AS KING

In the very first days of the world, when all the creatures were still learning to live together, they chose a king. Humans, animals and fish, all picked someone to lead them. But the birds of the Himalayas had no king. No leader to guide them, or settle their quarrels.

One morning, the birds gathered round, to choose a king. The birds flapped and chirped as they talked. 'Men have their king,' they said. 'Beasts have theirs. Even the fish in the sea do. But we birds have no leader. How can that be? We must find a king to watch over us. Someone strong. Someone wise.' In this life the Bodhisatta was born as a goose. He stood quietly among them, listening to their words, saying nothing.

After a lot of discussion and careful thinking, they decided that the owl would become the king of the birds. 'Here is the one we choose,' they said with hope. Soon, a call was sent across the mountains for all the birds to come and vote. They promised to ask three times, giving everyone a chance to say their piece. The

THE PET ELEPHANT

first two times, the birds listened quietly. Then, on the third call, a loud voice rose above the rest. It was the crow.

'Wait,' the crow said, hopping from branch to branch. 'Look at the owl's face, honoured and proud. But what will happen when he is angry? His sharp eyes could scare us all. We will scatter like dry leaves in the wind. I do not want this bird as our king!'

The birds hushed and looked at each other. The crow's words were sharp and clear. He warned them the owl's fierce face might bring fear instead of peace. Then the birds began chirping to one other.

Some birds were unsure. They wanted to believe the owl could be wise. But the crow's warning stirred doubts in many hearts.

Despite all the doubts, the birds chose the owl as their king. At first, everything seemed well. But soon, the owl's anger showed. When he was upset, he would shout at the other birds, and command them to do chores for him. His voice became harsh and sharp. The other birds began to fall silent. Some hid in the trees. Others dared not sing their songs or share their thoughts.

The forest, once full of happy chatter and music, grew silent and tense. Fear spread like a shadow under the owl's rule.

One day, the crow returned. He looked around at the other birds and said,

'I still don't agree with your choice.' The crow stood said, 'The owl is not fit to lead us. His angry eyes and sharp ways will only bring silence and fear, not peace.'

The owl, hearing this, was angry. He gave a low, grumbling hoot and flew after the crow, chasing him across the sky. Their

calls echoed like thunder, and from that day on, the owl and crow became enemies.

The Bodhisatta, watching all of this from afar, spoke to the birds who had gathered.

'We have to learn from all that has happened here. Power without compassion only brings harm. True strength is not found in sharp claws or loud voices, but in calm hearts and gentle hands. A real leader does not rule through fear. A real leader brings everyone together, with kindness, patience and care.'

After the owl flew away chasing the crow, The birds decided they needed a new king. They all agreed to choose Bodhisatta as their new king.

This story teaches us all: a leader must be chosen with wisdom. Anger and fear break bonds. Patience and kindness build them. The best king is the one who inspires trust, not dread.

18. THE FLIGHT OF THE BEASTS

Long ago, when King Brahmadatta ruled in the city of Benares, the Bodhisatta was born as a lion. He ruled over a lush green forest that stretched along the ocean's edge. He was wise and kind, and all the animals looked up to him. The animals lived peacefully under the tall vilva trees that shaded the forest. Among them was a small, curious hare who loved to rest in the cool shade.

One sunny afternoon, after nibbling on some fresh leaves, the little hare lay down beneath a huge vilva tree by the ocean. Suddenly, he had a scary thought. 'What if the earth suddenly breaks apart?' he wondered. At that very moment, a ripe vilva fruit fell from the tree and landed with a soft 'thud' on the forest floor.

Hearing the sound, the hare jumped up in fright. 'The earth is breaking!' he cried, and he ran away as fast as his little legs could carry him.

Another hare saw him running and asked, 'Why are you running in such a hurry? What's wrong?'

'Don't ask me!' replied the first hare, still trembling.

But the second hare was curious and chased after him. 'Please tell me. What scared you?'

The first hare stopped running but did not look back. 'The earth is breaking apart!' he said.

Terrified, the second hare took off running too. Soon, a third hare saw the panic and ran as well. One by one, hares from all over the forest began to flee.

The other animals saw this and asked, 'Why are all the hares running like that?'

The hare told them, 'The earth is breaking apart!'

Hearing this, the deer, boar, elk, buffalo, wild ox, rhinoceros, tiger and even the mighty elephant got scared. One after another, they joined the frantic flight.

The young lion watched all this and thought, 'The earth cannot be breaking apart. This must be a mistake. If I do not stop them, they will all be lost in fear.'

Quick as a flash, he ran ahead of the animals and reached the foot of a mountain. There, he roared loudly for all to hear. The animals stopped running and gathered around him, trembling.

'Why are you running away?' asked the lion.

'The earth is breaking!' they cried.

'Who saw it break?' the lion asked carefully.

'It was the hares,' said the animals, all at once.

The lion asked the hares, and they pointed to one hare who had started all the panic.

'Is it true the earth is breaking?' the lion asked the hare.

'Yes, I saw it,' the hare said.

'Where were you when it happened?' the lion asked.

THE FLIGHT OF THE BEASTS

'Near the ocean, in the grove of vilva trees,' the hare replied. 'I was resting under a tree when I heard a thud. I thought the earth was breaking, so I ran away.'

The lion smiled kindly. 'That thud was just a ripe fruit falling from the tree,' he explained. 'The earth is safe and sound.'

The lion took the hare and led the animals back to the grove. They saw the fallen fruit on the floor and understood the truth.

The animals calmed down and stopped running in fear. The lion told them, 'When you hear something frightening, don't let fear carry you away. Take a moment, stay calm and seek the truth before you decide what to believe.'

Thanks to the lion's wisdom and bravery, the animals were saved from blind fear. They learnt that sometimes fear can be caused by misunderstandings and that it is important to stay calm and look for the truth.

19. THE CAT AND THE CLEVER COCK

Just outside the city of Benares, a green forest hummed with the sounds of birds and rustling leaves. Among the busy birds was a special cock, full of courage and wisdom. He was the Bodhisatta, a gentle soul who helped all the animals with his quick thinking.

The forest was alive with the chatter and songs of many birds, but danger often lurked nearby. Not far away, in the shadows, lived a sly and cunning cat. She was known throughout the land for her trickery and cleverness in catching birds. She once pretended to cry near a bush, and when a kind little bird hopped over to ask what was wrong, she pounced on it. Another time, she rolled in dust and lay still like a rock. When a curious rabbit came close, she grabbed it in one quick leap. The creatures of the forest whispered stories about her tricks, but still some fell for them. One by one, she had managed to catch many of the cocks and other small animals that lived in the forest.

Despite all her tricks, she had never been able to catch the Bodhisatta. He was too smart and cautious. He always noticed her sneaky moves and escaped just in time.

THE CAT AND THE CLEVER COCK

The cat grew more and more frustrated. She decided that catching this clever cock would prove she was the smartest and most skilful of all the animals.

One morning, the cat made a plan to finally trap the cock. Instead of hiding and sneaking, she would use her words to trick the Bodhisatta. That cat licked her fur until it was smooth and shiny. She practised her voice, making it soft and sweet like a lullaby. Then she walked with careful steps to the Bodhisatta's tree, swinging her tail gently, like she meant no harm at all. She walked boldly to the tree where he liked to perch and called to him softly.

'Beautiful cock,' she said, 'you are the most graceful bird I have ever seen. Your feathers gleam in the sun, and your voice is the sweetest sound in the forest. Please come down from your tree and be my friend. Come along! We'll laugh, play and have all kinds of fun together.'

The Bodhisatta listened carefully to her words. He had seen many of his friends fall into the cat's traps before. He knew she was dangerous and could not be trusted. So he answered calmly, 'Dear cat, you may be clever, but I have wings and can fly. You have paws meant for hunting. Birds and beasts are not made to be friends or companions. It is better if you find someone who is more like you.'

The cat was surprised by his answer, but she did not give up so easily. She tried to sound kinder and more sincere, hoping to win his trust.

'If you come with me,' she said, 'I promise to bring you joy, happiness and kindness. You may treat me as your wife or servant. I will do anything you wish.'

The cock shook his head and replied firmly, 'I have seen how you have treated my friends and family. You have tricked

and eaten many of them. Your words are sweet, but your heart is not true. I cannot believe you.'

Hearing this, the cat realized her words would not fool the Bodhisatta. She felt defeated but knew she must leave before he flew away. Quietly, she slipped from the tree and disappeared into the forest.

Days passed, and the forest remained peaceful. The other cocks and animals heard what had happened and admired the Bodhisatta for his wisdom and bravery. They gathered around the Bodhisatta, and asked him how he had managed to outsmart the cat when so many others had been caught. The Bodhisatta smiled and said, 'The most important things are to be aware of those around you and to trust your instincts. When danger comes disguised as kindness, it is best to stay true to what you know.'

20. THE BRAVE WHITE HORSE AND THE GOBLIN CITY

On the island of Ceylon, there once stood a mysterious town called Sirisavatthu. Hidden behind its thick forests and tall cliffs, lived a band of hungry-eyed goblin women. These goblins lived there quietly, waiting for ships to wreck on the nearby shore.

Whenever a ship was broken by the sea, the goblin women would prepare carefully. Dressed in fine clothes, they would carry baskets filled with rice and gruel, all ready to welcome the shipwrecked sailors.

The sailors, exhausted and hungry after the wreckage, gladly accepted the food. They ate the rice and gruel, not knowing the danger lurking behind the friendly faces. After the meal, the goblins told a sorrowful tale of their own. 'Our husbands left us years ago on a ship and never came back,' they said. 'We have waited for them for so long and feel very lonely. We will be your wives and care for you.' Their words were gentle, and their smiles warm. Slowly, the sailors began to trust the goblins and followed them into the goblin city.

But once inside the city walls, the truth was revealed. The goblins trapped the sailors. Some were chained with magic and locked away in a dark cellar, trapped by powerful spells.

One time, five hundred sailors landed near the goblin city. The goblins welcomed them with the same tricks, made them their husbands and treated them kindly during the day. However, at night, the goblins revealed their evil face. The chief goblin and her followers set off to snatch away some of the sailors, and torture them.

Among the sailors, the eldest man began to notice something strange. That night, when the whole town was asleep, he was woken up by a low, grumbling whisper. It was like no voices he had heard before.

'That doesn't sound like any of the villagers.' He thought. 'Could it be ... goblins?'

He slipped quietly out of bed and hid behind a large stone. From there, he watched, careful not to make a sound. Before long, he saw the women walking through the town—only they no longer looked like women. In the moonlight, their shapes had changed. Their eyes gleamed, their teeth were sharp and their skin had turned blue. They were goblins, just as he had feared.

'We have been tricked.' He cried. 'We must escape before they hurt us all.'

Before the sun rose, he gathered some of the others. 'These women are goblins,' he said quietly. 'If we stay, they will capture and harm us. We must run away while there is still time.'

About half of the sailors agreed to escape with him. The rest were too afraid and chose to stay. The eldest sailor and two hundred and fifty others fled silently into the forest.

THE BRAVE WHITE HORSE AND THE GOBLIN CITY

Far above the island, a magical white horse soared through the sky. This was the Bodhisatta. He was strong and beautiful, with wide wings that carried him swiftly through the air. His beak was like that of a crow, and his mane shone like silver. He was known far and wide for his kindness and power.

As the magical horse flew, he called out in a gentle voice, 'What troubles you, kind men below?'

The sailors who had escaped heard his kind call. Hope filled their eyes. 'We want to go home, kind creature!' they shouted, 'We are being held by goblin women. They lured us in with their spells, and now we are trapped.'

'Come and climb on my back,' the horse said. Some climbed onto his wings, others held tightly to his tail, and a few stood and saluted him. With great care, the horse carried all two hundred and fifty sailors through the clouds, flying high above the island.

The magical horse gently placed each sailor safely where they belonged. He made sure no one fell or was hurt on the journey. After helping them all, the wise Bodhisatta told the sailors that danger can sometimes hide behind a friendly face. We must be careful and not trust everything we see. Then he returned to his home in the sky, proud that he had helped so many find their way back home.

21. THE CHAMELEON'S BETRAYAL

Long ago, in the forest near the great city of Benares, a very wise lizard lived on the banks of a river. It was the Bodhisatta, who had been born as the king of hundreds of lizards. They all lived together in a burrow deep in the earth.

The Bodhisatta had a son, a cheerful young lizard who loved to play. One day, the young prince made friends with a chameleon. The two were always together, chasing ants, curling their tails around twigs and playing hide-and-seek among the rocks. The young lizard hugged his friend often, curling around him in a great scaly squeeze.

When the Bodhisatta heard of this friendship, he grew concerned. He called his son and said gently, 'My dear, chameleons are not wise friends. They change their colours and minds too easily. One day, this friendship may bring trouble to us all.'

But the young lizard smiled and said, 'Father, he is kind to me. We play every day. He would never hurt me.'

THE CHAMELEON'S BETRAYAL

Still, the Bodhisatta warned him again, but the son did not listen. Quietly, the Bodhisatta ordered a second tunnel to be dug, a hidden back exit to their burrow. He knew that wisdom meant preparing, even when others ignored the danger.

Seasons passed. The young lizard grew large and strong, while the chameleon stayed small. As they played, the lizard's friendly hugs became heavy and painful. The chameleon winced and thought, 'If this continues, I will be squashed to death.'

Angry and sore, the chameleon came up with a wicked plan. He would lead a hunter to the lizards' burrow and destroy them once and for all.

One summer day, after a heavy storm, ants came crawling out of the ground, and the lizards danced in delight, darting out to eat them. Just then, a hunter entered the forest with dogs and a spade. He was looking for lizards to catch.

The chameleon approached him, his voice sweet and sly. 'Good sir, if you want lizards, I know where to find hundreds. Follow me.'

The hunter looked surprised. 'Do you really?'

'Yes,' said the chameleon. 'Bring fire and your dogs. I will show you the way.'

He led the hunter to the burrow and said, 'Fill this tunnel with smoke. When the lizards come running out, strike them with your stick. Your dogs can catch the rest.'

Then he crawled up onto a nearby rock and puffed out his chest, watching the scenes unfold below.

The hunter followed the plan. He lit firewood and pushed it into the tunnel. Thick smoke filled the burrow. Inside, the lizards began to cough and panic. Blinded by the smoke, they rushed towards the only entrance.

As they came out gasping, the hunter swung his stick. If he missed, the dogs chased and caught them. Many lizards lost their lives that day.

The Bodhisatta realised what had happened. He saw the chameleon watching with narrowed eyes and understood the truth. Without panic, he led the remaining lizards through the secret tunnel he had prepared. They escaped into the forest and hid in safety. The lizards were shaken. They had lost many of their family. That evening, the Bodhisatta gathered them under a tree. The younger ones huddled close, their tails trembling. He cried out to them, 'This is what happens when we make friends with the untrustworthy. One false friend can bring down a hundred honest hearts. We must never forget that wisdom keeps us safe. Not every smiling face brings good intentions.'

The young lizard sat beside his father, his head bowed. He was quiet for a long time, then whispered, 'I'm sorry, Father. I should have listened.'

The Bodhisatta placed his tail gently around his son. 'We learn by falling,' he said. 'But now you know to look more closely. Kindness is good, but it must be wise. Friendship with someone who lies, cheats, or changes his ways can only bring ruin.'

From that day on, the lizards lived more carefully. And the chameleon, left alone on his rock, never found another friend.

22. THE TREE THAT TOLD A LIE

Not far from the bustling city of Benares, a boy was born into a wealthy merchant's family. His parents named him 'Wise' because he was unusually brilliant, right from a very young age. He was the Bodhisatta. As Wise grew up, he became a fair and successful merchant. One day, he began trading with another man who called himself 'Wisest'. This man was proud, always praising himself and boasting to others. But Wise, true to his name, stayed humble and gentle. Together, they loaded five hundred wagons with fine goods and set off to trade in the countryside.

The journey was long. They stopped at many villages, setting out silk cloth, copper pots and colourful beads. Children gathered to look, their eyes wide with curiosity. Wise spoke politely to each customer and offered fair prices. Wisest, on the other hand, always tried to charge more, even when buyers looked unsure. 'A clever trader must be quick and bold!' he said. But Wise replied, 'A good trader is fair and honest.' Bit by bit, the wagons emptied, and their sacks filled with coins.

When the time came to divide their earnings, Wisest crossed his arms and declared, 'I should get two shares.'

Wise blinked. 'Why would you get more than me?'

'Because I am Wisest. That makes me twice as clever. And cleverness earns more.'

Wise frowned but spoke calmly. 'We worked equally. We travelled together, sold together and faced the same hardships. That makes us equal partners.'

But Wisest would not agree. 'If you think I'm wrong, let's ask the tree spirit. Let the spirit judge.'

Now, Wisest had planned a trick. He had told his old father to hide inside a large hollow tree near the edge of the forest. The tree stood tall and still as they stepped before it.

Wisest bowed deeply. 'O great tree spirit, please help us. I am Wisest and this is Wise. We shared our trade. Tell us, how should the treasure be divided?'

From within the trunk came a deep, rumbling voice. 'Give one share to Wise and two to Wisest.'

Wise looked at the tree and narrowed his eyes in suspicion. Something was not right. The voice did not sound like a spirit. To find out the truth behind the magical tree spirit, he picked up some dry straw and gently placed it in the hollow of the tree. With a flick of flint and stone, he lit a small flame.

Wisest watched nervously. 'What are you doing?' he asked, his voice a little too loud.

Wise didn't answer. Smoke began to curl from the hollow, soft at first, then in thick, grey clouds. The tree's branches rustled. The trunk gave a sudden shake. And then a sound came from inside the tree.

'Help! Help! I'm in here!'

THE TREE THAT TOLD A LIE

With a great cough and a burst of smoke, an old man leapt out of the tree, waving his arms and blinking through the ash. His hair was singed, and his robes were smudged with soot.

'I can't take it anymore!' he cried. 'I'm not a spirit! I'm just a foolish old man helping his son cheat an honest friend! Forgive me, Wise. This was not your fault, and you did not deserve such trickery.' He gasped. 'Because of my son's trick, I've nearly been roasted in a flame!'

The truth was out. Wisest turned red with shame and looked down. The Bodhisatta, however, did not scold or shout. He looked at him gently and said, 'Let us divide everything fairly. One half each. That is what is right.'

So, they counted every coin and split the wagons evenly. There was no anger, no punishment, only justice. The people watching were amazed. They whispered to one another, 'This is true wisdom, to act kindly even when wronged.'

As Wise walked home, the wind cooled his face and the sun warmed the path. He thought to himself, 'Cleverness without truth is like a tree without roots. It may look grand, but it cannot stand for long.'

23. THE CARPENTER, THE SON AND THE BODHISATTA

In a peaceful village near the borders of Kasi, the air always smelled of fresh wood and pine. The sound of hammers tapping and saws scraping filled the small workshops where carpenters worked.

In one workshop, an old carpenter sat on his bench. His head was bald and shiny like a polished bowl. He was working a piece of teak wood. The blade moved steadily, making a soft scratching noise as it smoothed the wood. A pile of shavings had gathered by his feet. He paused now and then to check the shape with his fingers, then kept going. Outside, the sound of children shouting drifted in through the open door, but he paid no attention.

Beside him, his son sat quietly, carving a small wooden bird with careful hands. His brow was furrowed in concentration, copying each movement just as he had seen his father do.

Suddenly, a tiny mosquito settled on the carpenter's bare head. It was no bigger than a speck of dust but its sting was

THE CARPENTER, THE SON AND THE BODHISATTA

sharp like a needle. The old man flinched and rubbed the back of his head with a slow hand.

'My boy,' he said to his son, 'there is a mosquito biting me on the head. Please get rid of it.'

The son looked up, calm and steady. He put down his carving knife and stood up. 'Hold still, Father,' he said. 'I will drive it away with one quick blow.'

At that moment, the Bodhisatta came into the workshop. He was travelling through the village as a trader. People knew him for his wisdom and gentle heart. He sat quietly in the corner, watching what was happening.

The son picked up a sharp axe. The blade shone in the sunlight like silver. He raised it carefully, aiming for the tiny mosquito resting on his father's head. His heart was kind and full of good will. He wanted to help his father.

But in his eagerness, the son struck too hard.

With a terrible crack, the axe missed the mosquito and hit the old man's head instead. The sound was awful and sudden. The carpenter fell down, still and silent.

The son froze, his eyes wide with shock. Tears began to fall down his cheeks. 'Father!' he cried, kneeling beside the fallen man.

The Bodhisatta stood and walked over. His face was calm but his eyes showed sadness. He gently put his hand on the son's shoulder.

'Your heart is kind,' he said softly, 'but your action was not wise. It is better to have an enemy who understands what he is doing than a friend who harms without meaning to.'

He looked around so everyone could hear his words.

'When we care for others, we must act with both kindness

and wisdom. To strike without thought, even with good intention, can bring great sorrow.'

The villagers listened quietly. The son wept bitterly for his father and for his mistake. The village mourned the loss of the carpenter.

The Bodhisatta continued, 'Love without care can be dangerous. When you want to help, you must think carefully and act with understanding. Wisdom guides kindness so it does no harm.'

24. COURAGE AND KINDNESS

In the great city of Benares, a very special prince was born. This prince was the Bodhisatta. His name was Prince Goodness because he showed kindness and fairness to everyone around him.

From when he was a little boy, Prince Goodness loved all creatures and learnt everything needed to be a good leader. When his father, the king, passed away, Prince Goodness became the new king. People called him King Goodness because he ruled with love and justice.

King Goodness cared deeply for his people. He built almonries where travellers and poor people could find food and shelter. He was patient and gentle, like a father caring for his children. The city was peaceful, and everyone respected their king.

But not everyone was good. One of the king's ministers was found to be corrupt. When King Goodness found out, he was sad but did what was right. He told the minister to leave the kingdom and take his family away. The minister left the country angry and humiliated. Seeking revenge, he went to a neighbouring king, the king of Kosala.

This minister told the king of Kosala that Benares was weak and easy to take over. The king of Kosala did not believe this at first. To test if it was true, he sent groups of men to cause trouble in Benares. These men made their way to Benares and ransacked a village, killing some of the villagers as they went. After causing much havoc, the men were caught and brought before King Goodness.

The king asked them, 'Tell me, why have you killed my villagers?' 'Kind king, We have no food or work. Said the men 'It was hunger that drove us to do it'. The king showed kindness. Instead of punishing them, he told them not to hurt anyone ever again and sent them away with gifts. The king of Kosala heard this but still wanted to take over the kingdom.

Soon, the king of Kosala came with his army to Benares. The soldiers of King Goodness wanted to fight to protect their home, but the king said no. He told them not to cause harm because he wanted to rule with peace. The king of Kosala entered the city without a fight. The doors were open, and King Goodness sat calmly on his throne.

The king of Kosala was cruel. He ordered his soldiers to tie up King Goodness and his ministers. They buried them up to their necks in a dark, lonely cemetery pit. But even then, King Goodness did not feel anger or fear. He told his friends to stay kind and hopeful.

At night, wild jackals came to the pit, hoping to find food. The king bit one of the jackals on the throat so hard that it howled loudly. The other jackals ran away, scared. The trapped jackal struggled and loosened the earth covering King Goodness.

COURAGE AND KINDNESS

Using all his strength, King Goodness pulled himself out of the pit. Finally free, he pulled his ministers out of the ground.

Nearby, two goblins were arguing over a dead body. They asked King Goodness to settle their quarrel. 'Wise king, settle this for us—who should get the body?' said one. The king replied, 'I will settle your quarrel, but allow me to clean myself first.' Using their magic, the goblins brought him scented water, fine clothes and delicious food.

Once ready, King Goodness cut the dead body in two and gave each goblin their share. The goblins were grateful and offered to help the king. The king asked them to take him to the chamber of the king of Kosala, and his ministers back to their homes.

That night, while the king of Kosala was sleeping peacefully, King Goodness appeared by his bedside and tapped him lightly on the belly with his sword. He woke up in surprise and listened as King Goodness told him what had happened.

The king of Kosala was amazed by the king's goodness and bravery. He said, 'Kind king, I didn't see your kindness, though even the wild goblins did. I promise never to plot against you again.' From that day on, the two kings agreed to live in peace, and King Goodness ruled his kingdom once more.

25. THE CLEVER CRAB AND THE CRANE

Near a quiet forest, there was a small pond, peaceful and clear, with lotus flowers blooming on its surface. Dragonflies zipped back and forth, their wings catching the light in flashes of blue and green. Frogs croaked softly from beneath broad lily pads. Below the water's surface, silver fish weaved gracefully among the roots of floating lotuses.

Standing tall by the edge of the pond was a mighty tree. Its branches stretched wide, full of thick, green leaves. This was no ordinary tree. It was the Bodhisatta, who had taken this form to watch over the pond and all the beings who lived there. From his high branches, the Bodhisatta saw everything. He listened to the birds singing and watched the creatures moving below with calm, gentle eyes.

That summer, the sun burnt hotter than ever before. Day after day, the air shimmered with heat, and the pond's water began to shrink. The silver fish swam faster, searching for cooler spots. The frogs grew quiet, hiding beneath lily pads. The

THE CLEVER CRAB AND THE CRANE

pond was becoming smaller and warmer, and the fish started to worry. Their home was changing, and soon it might disappear.

One morning, a crane appeared in the pond. He stood silently by the water's edge, his long legs dipping into the cool pond. The fish noticed him and gathered near the surface.

'Why do you watch us so quietly, Crane?' asked a small silver fish, flicking his tail.

The crane lifted his head and spoke softly, 'It's a scorching summer this year. This pond is drying up. Soon, there will be no space left for you to swim, no cool water to hide in. But not far from here is a large lake, filled with fresh water and blooming lotuses. It would be a safe home for you.'

The fish listened carefully, dreaming of cool water to swim in.

'But how can we trust you?' said a shy goldfish. 'No crane has ever helped fish before.'

The crane smiled gently. 'Send one of your own with me,' he said. 'I will carry your friend to the lake and bring him back safely.'

After a moment, a large, brave fish with one cloudy eye volunteered. The crane bent down and gently picked up the fish in his beak. Higher and higher they flew, the cool breeze rushing past them. The fish looked down at the shrinking pond and the tall trees beyond.

At last, the crane set the one-eyed fish down in a cool corner of the lake. The fish looked around. The water was clear and cool. The lotuses bloomed in pink and white, their sweet scent filling the air. The fish swam happily in the new home, then the crane picked him up again and carried him back.

The one-eyed fish told the others all about the beautiful lake. Slowly, one by one, the crane carried more fish away

from the pond. The silver fish went first, then the goldfish and even the tiny minnows followed. All of them left with hope in their hearts.

But something was wrong.

Instead of flying straight to the lake, the crane stopped near a tall tree. There, hidden among the branches, he dashed each fish against the bark and ate them. Then one after the other, he picked all the fish of the pond and took them to the tree, and then feasted on the easy meal. Bones piled up beneath the tree.

Back in the pond, only a clever crab remained. He watched the crane with sharp eyes as he came to the water's edge.

'Come with me to the lake,' said the crane.

'How will you carry me?' asked the crab, raising one claw.

'In my beak,' said the crane.

'If you'll let me hold your neck with my claws, I will come,' said the crab confidently.

The crane agreed, and the two rose into the air.

As they flew, the crab looked down. The tall tree was growing closer. The crane was not going to the lake. The crab's claws tightened around the crane's neck.

'You tricked the others,' said the crab firmly. 'I will not be fooled.' With all his strength, the crab squeezed. The crane gasped and lost control. He fell to the ground with a heavy thud.

From his branches, the Bodhisatta sighed softly.

'Those who deceive others will find their own plans undone,' he said. 'But those who are wise and brave will find safety and peace.'

The crab carefully crawled back to the pond. The fish who remained learnt the lesson that one should trust only those with good hearts.